Get Crafty Outdoors

Science and Craft Projects with

PLANTS
AND SEEDS

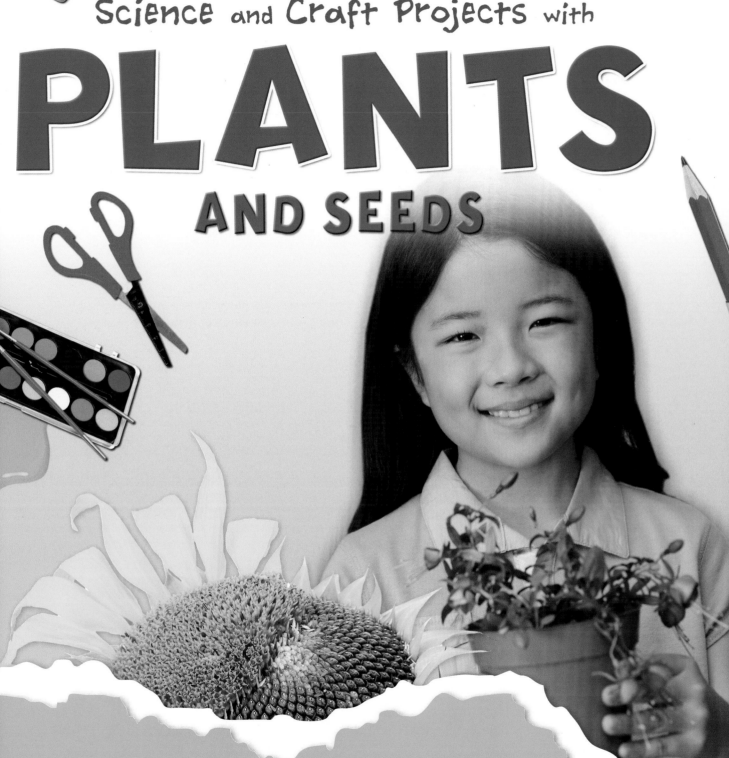

by Ruth Owen

PowerKiDS press.

New York

Published in 2013 by The Rosen Publishing Group, Inc.
29 East 21st Street, New York, NY 10010

Produced for Rosen by Ruby Tuesday Books Ltd
Editor for Ruby Tuesday Books Ltd: Mark J. Sachner
US Editor: Sara Antill
Designer: Emma Randall
Consultant: Suzy Gazlay

Photo credits:
Cover, 1, 4–5, 6 (right), 7, 8–9, 10–11, 14–15, 16–17, 18, 20–21, 22–23, 24, 25 (top), 26–27 © Shutterstock; 6 (left) © Steve Renich, Wikipedia Creative Commons; 12–13, 25 (bottom), 28–29 © Ruby Tuesday Books Ltd; 19 © Wikipedia Creative Commons.

Library of Congress Cataloging-in-Publication Data

Owen, Ruth, 1967–
 Science and craft projects with plants and seeds / by Ruth Owen.
    pages cm. — (Get crafty outdoors)
 Includes index.
 ISBN 978-1-4777-0247-5 (library binding) — ISBN 978-1-4777-0257-4 (pbk.) —
 ISBN 978-1-4777-0258-1 (6-pack)
 1. Nature craft—Juvenile literature. I. Title.
 TT160.O845 2013
 745.5—dc23
                                   2012033427

Manufactured in the United States of America

CPSIA Compliance Information: Batch #W13PK7: For Further Information contact Rosen Publishing, New York, New York at 1-800-237-9932

Contents

The Amazing World of Plants

There are nearly half a million different types of plants on Earth. Plants can be huge, like a tree, or tiny, like a **weed** growing in a sidewalk.

a tree

a dandelion weed

Plants live in many different **habitats**, from hot, dry **deserts** to the cold and windy Arctic **tundra**.

Inside this book, you will find out lots of facts about plants. You can also learn how some plants **reproduce**, or make new plants, by growing **seeds**. There are also six fun plant craft projects to make!

stems

a saguaro cactus

Plants for Hot, Plants for Cold

Saguaro cacti grow in a desert habitat where very little rain falls. If it does rain, a saguaro sucks up water through its roots and stores it in its fleshy stems. Pasqueflowers grow on the Arctic tundra. These plants are covered with hairs as protection against the cold.

hairs

pasqueflower

All About Plant Parts

switchgrass

roots

The roots on this switchgrass plant are 10 feet (3 m) long.

Plants come in many different sizes and shapes but most plants have the same parts.

leaves

Plants suck up water and **nutrients** from the soil through their roots.

A plant's roots grow down into the soil and hold a plant steady so it doesn't fall over. Roots can be as thin as a hair or thicker than a person's arm!

A plant's main stem grows from its roots and connects to thinner stems. The stems carry water and nutrients from the roots to the rest of the plant.

thinner stem

main stem

roots

Some plants have flowers where the plants' seeds are made.

stigma

style

anther

filament

petal

stem

leaf

The World's Biggest Flower

The plant with the biggest flower in the world is the *rafflesia arnoldii*. Rafflesias grow in rain forests on the Asian islands of Borneo and Sumatra. The flower of the *rafflesia arnoldii* can grow to be 3 feet (1 m) wide!

Pressed Flowers

By pressing flowers using a heavy book, you can make flower pictures that will last forever! You will have to be a little patient to make this craft, but the results are worth it.

You will need:

- Fresh flowers and leaves
- Waxed paper
- One large, heavy book
- Several other heavy books

- Colorful construction paper or thin cardboard
- Glue
- An adult to be your teammate and go flower gathering with you

Get Crafty:

1 Before you gather your flowers and leaves, make sure you ask permission from the person who owns the plants. If you cannot pick flowers in a garden you can use store-bought flowers instead.

2 Pick some flower heads and leaves that look fresh and colorful. Make sure the flowers are not wet when you pick them. Go onto step 3 as quickly as possible so the flowers are as fresh as possible when you press them.

3 Place the large, heavy book on a flat surface and open it. Lay a piece of waxed paper on the right-hand page.

4 Lay some flowers and leaves on the waxed paper.

5 Cover the flowers with another sheet of waxed paper. Then close the book.

6 Now open the book in another place and repeat steps 3 to 5. Keep doing this until you have used up all your flowers and leaves.

7 Put the heavy book in a place where it will not be disturbed, and put the other books on top of it to add weight.

8 Now comes the waiting part! You will need to wait for two weeks. In that time, the flowers will dry out and become flat, so you can use them to make pictures.

Happy Mother's Day

9 When it's time to look at your flowers, carefully open the pages of the book. The flowers will be delicate, so handle them carefully.

10 Glue the pressed flowers and leaves to construction paper or cardboard to make pictures and greetings cards.

Making Seeds

Before a flowering plant can make seeds, its flowers must be **pollinated**. Many flowers need help from insects and other small animals for this to happen.

Flowers produce a dust called **pollen** on their **anthers**.

orange pollen

anther

stigma

butterfly

bee

white pollen

Pollinators

When an animal, such as a bee or butterfly, visits a flower, some pollen sticks to the animal's body.

Then the bee flies off and visits a different flower of the same kind. Some of the pollen on the animal's body brushes off and sticks to that flower's **stigma**.

The flower with pollen on its stigma is now pollinated and can begin to make seeds.

Animals that move pollen from flower to flower on their bodies are called pollinators. Insects such as bees, butterflies, and beetles are pollinators. So are some types of birds and bats. Most pollinators visit flowers to feed on a sweet liquid called nectar that flowers produce.

anthers

a hummingbird drinking nectar

Butterfly Clips

In spring and summer keep watch for butterflies visiting flowers to drink nectar. Then make your own collection of colorful butterfly clips using wooden clothespins.

You will need:

- Wooden clothespins
- Colorful construction paper or thin cardboard
- Scissors
- Colored markers or pens
- Glue
- Pipe cleaners
- Peel and stick goggly eyes
- An adult to be your teammate and help with cutting

Get Crafty:

1 Draw the shape of four wings on the cardboard or construction paper. Ask an adult to help you cut them out.

2 Decorate the wings with spots, stripes, or other patterns.

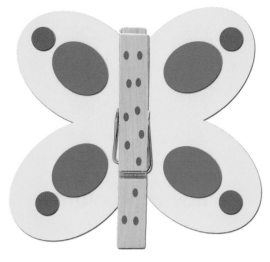

3 Glue the wings to the back of a wooden clothespin.

4 Draw stripes, spots, or other patterns on the clothespin to make the butterfly's body.

5 Bend a pipe cleaner into a V-shape. Then bend the ends into spirals to make the butterfly's antennae. Glue the antennae between the two halves of the clothespin.

6 Stick the goggly eyes to the butterfly's head.

7 Your butterfly clip is ready to use to hold photographs or important messages. You can also make butterfly clips to give as gifts!

Swimming
Monday

All About Seeds

After a flowering plant has been pollinated, the plant's seeds begin to form inside the flowers.

Seeds can be as tiny as grains of sand, or bigger than your head!

A flowering plant's seeds grow inside a protective case, or covering, called a fruit.

a poppy seedpod, or fruit

dying flower

a dried poppy seedpod

poppy flower

poppy seeds

watermelon

You might think of a fruit as being an apple or a peach. A fruit, however, is any kind of outer layer that protects seeds as they grow.

Some fruits, such as melons, tomatoes, or bean pods, are soft. Others, such as acorns, are hard. Inside an acorn is a seed that can grow into a new oak tree.

seeds

bean seeds

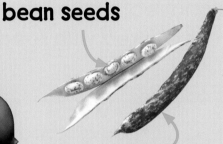

acorns

bean pod

tomato seeds

Seeds from Cones

Plants without flowers grow their seeds in other ways. Pine trees grow their seeds inside cones. When the seeds are fully grown, the pinecone's scales open up so the seeds can fall out.

pinecone

open scales

scales

pine tree seeds

Make a Giant Sunflower

Use your own handprints and real sunflower seeds to make a giant flower with a center packed with seeds.

You will need:

- Yellow finger paint
- A flat dish or container
- Large sheet of white construction paper
- Scissors
- A saucer
- A pencil

- A piece of black cardboard approximately 10 inches by 10 inches (25 cm x 25 cm)
- Glue (choose a clear glue)
- Sunflower seeds in shells or kernels
- An adult to be your teammate and help with cutting

Get Crafty:

1 Ask an adult to help you pour the paint into the flat container.

2 On the large piece of construction paper make 10 or 12 paint handprints. When the handprints are dry, ask an adult to help you cut out them out.

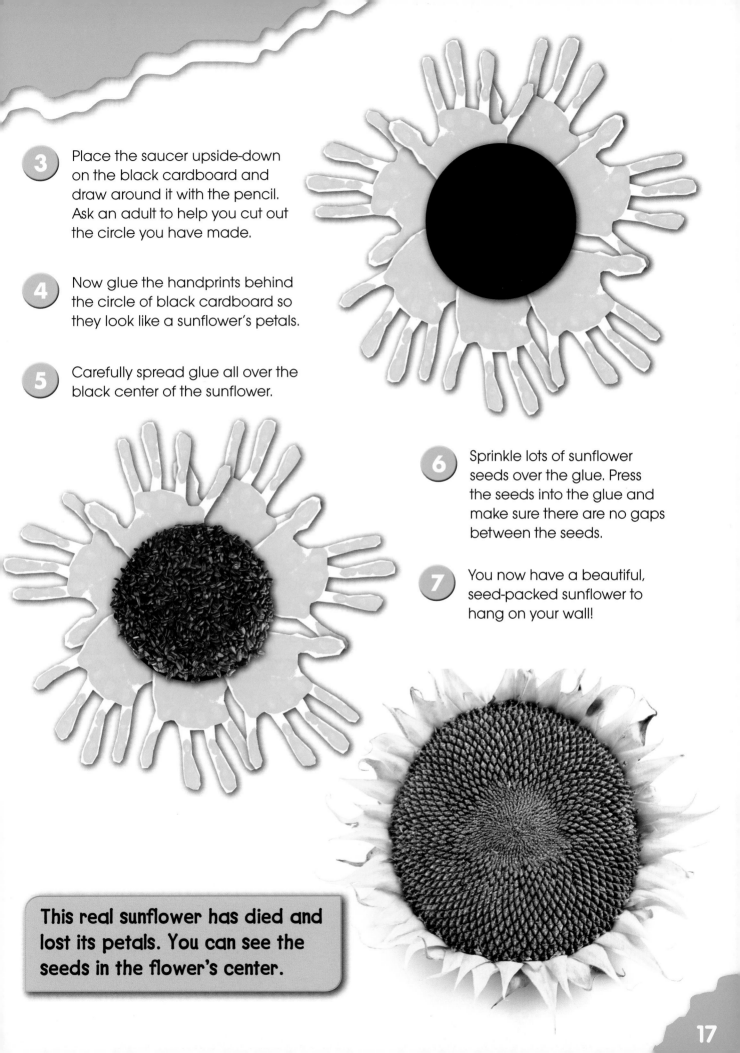

3. Place the saucer upside-down on the black cardboard and draw around it with the pencil. Ask an adult to help you cut out the circle you have made.

4. Now glue the handprints behind the circle of black cardboard so they look like a sunflower's petals.

5. Carefully spread glue all over the black center of the sunflower.

6. Sprinkle lots of sunflower seeds over the glue. Press the seeds into the glue and make sure there are no gaps between the seeds.

7. You now have a beautiful, seed-packed sunflower to hang on your wall!

This real sunflower has died and lost its petals. You can see the seeds in the flower's center.

A New Plant

Once a seed is fully grown and ripe, it is ready to leave its parent plant. A bean seed falls from its parent plant when the bean pod splits open.

bean seeds

Most seeds ripen in summer and fall. Once they are settled in some soil, they wait for spring before starting to grow.

First, roots grow from the seed into the soil. Then a shoot, or seedling, grows above ground.

The seedling has been taking water and nutrients from the soil through its little roots. Now it also needs sunlight to grow.

Soon, tiny leaves sprout from the seedling. Then the seedling grows and grows to become a plant.

shoot or seedling

stem

leaf

bean seed

roots

redwood trees

Tiny Seeds, Giant Plants

Redwood trees are the tallest plants in the world. A redwood seed, however, is not much bigger than a grain of rice. It takes hundreds of years, but a tiny seed may grow into a redwood tree that is as tall as a 30-story building!

Seed Mosaics

A mosaic is a picture made from hundreds or thousands of tiny pieces of paper, fabric, tile, or stone. Seeds come in so many different colors that they are a great material for making mosaic pictures, too. Get creative and make some seed mosaics using dried beans and other seeds!

You will need:

- A selection of dried seeds
- Small bowls
- Black or white thin cardboard
- A pencil
- Glue (choose a clear glue)

Get Crafty:

 Put all your different seeds into individual bowls.

green peas

yellow split peas

red kidney beans

chickpeas

pinto beans

black beans

broad beans

red lentils

 Decide what type of picture you want to make. You can write your name, create a landscape scene, or make patterns.

3 First, draw your design on a piece of cardboard.

4 Spread glue in a small section of your picture. Sprinkle seeds over the glue so that the whole section is thickly covered with seeds.

5 Now spread glue in another section. Keep working on your picture section by section.

6 Once you've finished your picture, leave it lying flat until the glue has completely dried. Have fun!

7 You can draw shapes and fill them with different seeds to make patterns (like the circle below). You can even make a seed mosaic frame for a favorite photograph.

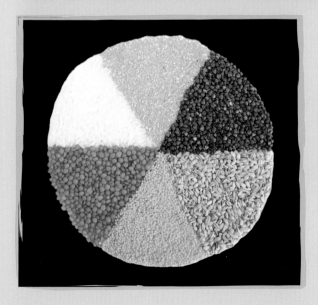

A Good Place to Grow

If a seed tries to grow in the soil close to its parent plant there may not be enough water and nutrients to go around. Also, the bigger plant may block out the sunlight. So many types of seeds move to new growing places away from their parent plants.

seeds

Some seeds get moved to new places in the stomachs of animals!

A bird might eat some fruit with seeds inside. Then the bird will fly off to a new place with the seeds in its stomach. The seeds will be released into the new place with the bird's waste.

papaya fruit

This horse has burdock seeds stuck in its mane.

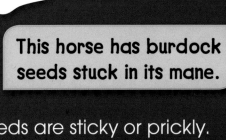

Some seeds are sticky or prickly. These seeds can become attached to the fur of animals and get carried to a new place to grow.

seeds

Flying Seeds

Dandelion seeds are blown to new growing places by the wind. Each dandelion seed is attached to a tiny fluffy parachute that catches the wind and helps the seed float away from its parent plant.

dandelion

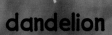

Make a Waxy Dandelion Picture

Wax and paint don't mix. You can use the effect they create together to make a beautiful picture of a dandelion.

You will need:

- White paper
- Paint
- Paintbrushes
- A white wax crayon
- A black marker pen
- A magnifying glass

dandelion seed head

seed

parachute

Get Crafty:

1 Before you start on your artwork, take a close look at the dandelion seed head in this picture. Better still, if it is spring, summer, or fall, try to find a real dandelion seed head.

2 Try using a magnifying glass to study a dandelion's tiny black seeds and their fluffy parachutes.

3 To make your picture, draw a fluffy dandelion seed head with the white crayon. Draw the fluffy parachute parts of the seeds floating in the air, too.

4 With the black marker, add black dots for seeds attached to each of the parachutes.

5 Now comes the really amazing part. Cover the whole picture with blue paint. The wax will resist, or throw off, the paint and the areas on the paper where you drew the dandelions in crayon will remain white!

6 You can try different designs using this effect. For example, use the crayon to draw lots of dandelions on the ground and white, fluffy clouds in the sky.

Food from Plants

Plants don't just make our world look beautiful. Without plants to eat, people and all the other animals on Earth could not survive!

People eat plants when they eat vegetables, fruits, and seeds.

Rice is a type of seed.

Carrots are actually the thick, orange root of a carrot plant!

When we eat lettuce, we are eating leaves!

Grains such as wheat are grass plants that we use to make flour. Delicious foods such as bread, cakes, cookies, and pancakes are all made from flour.

wheat   flour

dairy cow

You might think you could survive by eating only hamburgers or sausage. These foods would not exist without plants, however. That's because meat comes from plant-eating animals such as cattle and pigs.

No Ice Cream Without Plants!

Without plants, we wouldn't have milk, or foods made from milk such as cheese and ice cream. That's because we get milk from dairy cows or goats that eat grass and other plants. It's possible to make milk in other ways, but not without plants. Soy milk and rice milk are both made from plants!

Create a Fruit T-shirt

Fruits and vegetables aren't just good to eat. These plant foods can also be used to print shapes. In this project, you can give a T-shirt a cool new look using designs made from pieces of fruits and veggies!

You will need:

- A plain T-shirt
- Fabric paints (ask an adult to read the packaging of the fabric paint to check if there are any special instructions before you begin work)
- Dishes (one for each paint color)
- Paintbrushes
- Your choice of fruits and vegetables
- A cutting board
- A knife
- Paper
- An adult to be your teammate and help with cutting the fruits and vegetables

Get Crafty:

1. Pour the paints into the dishes.

2. Now ask an adult to help you cut up the fruits and vegetables. To create a design on your T-shirt you will be dipping the pieces of fruits and vegetables into the paints.

Fruits such as apples, oranges, and lemons can be cut in half to make patterns like this.

  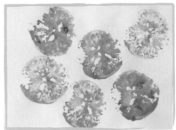 

Pieces of broccoli make pretty, fluffy patterns.

Trim off the base of a romaine lettuce. Its pattern looks like a flower.

Put pieces of corn onto skewers. These can be rolled onto paper or fabric.

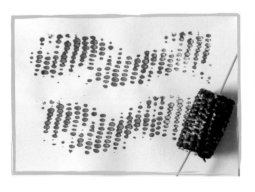

3 Try out some ideas and designs on paper before you begin work on your T-shirt.

4 Once you have decided on a design, get crafty on your T-shirt. Dip a piece of fruit or vegetable into the paint, or use a paintbrush to cover it with paint. Then press the shape onto the fabric.

5 When you have finished your design, allow the paint to dry. Then follow any special final instructions on the packaging of the fabric paint.

Glossary

anther (AN-thur)
The part of a flower that produces pollen.

desert (DEH-zurt)
A dry, rocky, or sandy habitat where very little rain or snow falls and few plants can grow. Some deserts are very hot, while others are very cold.

habitat (HA-buh-tat)
The place where an animal or plant normally lives. A habitat may be a backyard, a forest, the ocean, or a pond in a park.

nutrients (NOO-tree-ents)
Substances needed by a plant or animal to help it live and grow. Animals get nutrients, such as vitamins, from their food, while plants get nutrients from the soil.

pollen (PAH-lin)
A colored dust made on the anthers of flowers, which plants need in order to reproduce.

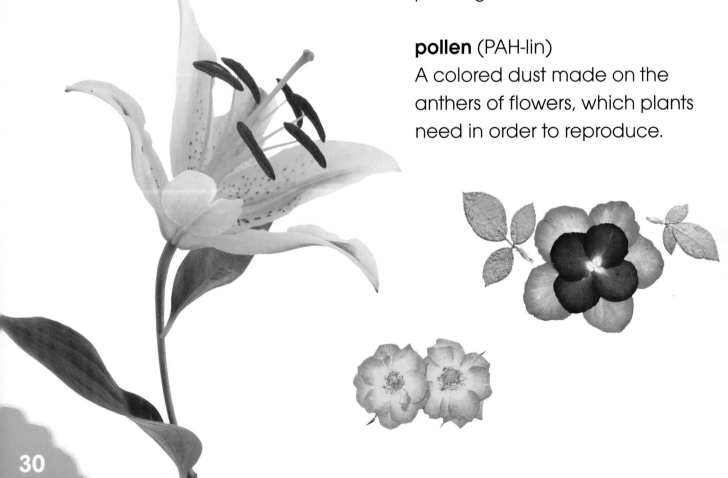

pollinated (PAH-luh-nayt-ed)
When pollen is carried from the anthers of a flower to the stigma. Pollen can be moved between these parts on the same plant or to a different plant of the same kind.

reproduce (ree-pruh-DOOS)
To make more of something, such as when plants make seeds or animals mate in order to produce young.

ripe (RYP)
Fully grown and ready to leave a parent plant.

seed (SEED)
A part of a plant that contains all the material needed to grow a new plant.

stigma (STIG-muh) The part, or parts, of a flower where pollen must land in order for pollination to happen so that a flower can begin to make seeds.

tundra (TUN-druh) The frozen land of the coldest parts of the world.

weed (WEED) A plant growing where it is not wanted. Weeds are often tough, wild plants that grow very quickly.

Websites

Due to the changing nature of Internet links, PowerKids Press has developed an online list of websites related to the subject of this book. This site is updated regularly. Please use this link to access the list:
www.powerkidslinks.com/gco/plant/

Read More

Peterson, Cris. *Seed, Soil, Sun: Earth's Recipe for Food*. Honesdale, PA: Boyds Mills Press, 2011.

Rhodes, Evan. *How Do Seeds Sprout?*. Nature's Super Secrets. New York: Gareth Stevens, 2013.

Thomson, Ruth. *A Sunflower's Life Cycle*. Let's Look at Life Cycles. New York: PowerKids Press, 2010.

Index